Book Publishing for Beginners:

How to have a successful book launch and market your self-published book to a #1 bestseller and grow your business

By

Paul G. Brodie

Book Publishing for Beginners: How to have a successful book launch and market your self-published book to a #1 bestseller and grow your business

Copyright @ 2016 by Paul G. Brodie

Editing by Devin Rene Hacker

Published in the United States by BrodieEDU Publishing, 2016.

Disclaimer

The following viewpoints in this book are those of Paul Brodie. These views are based on his personal experience over the past forty years on the planet Earth, especially while living in the great state of Texas.

The intention of this book is to share his stories of both success and struggles with book publishing and what has worked for *him* through this journey.

All attempts have been made to verify the information provided by this publication. Neither the author nor the publisher assumes any responsibility for errors, omissions, or contrary interpretations of the subject matter herein.

This book is for entertainment purposes only. The views expressed are those of the author alone and should not be taken as expert instruction or commands. The reader is responsible for his or her future action. This book makes no guarantees of future income. However by following the steps that are listed in this book the odds of increased revenue streams for your future book launches definitely have a much higher probability.

Neither the author nor the publisher assume any responsibility or liability on the behalf of the purchaser or reader of these materials.

The views expressed are based on his personal experiences within the corporate world, education, and everyday life.

This book is dedicated to my mom, Barbara "Mama" Brodie. Without her support and motivation (and incredible cooking) I would literally not be here today

Contents

Free Audiobook Offer

Are you a fan of audiobooks? I would like to offer you the audiobook of Motivation 101 for free. All you need to do is go to my website at www.BrodieEDU.com/freeaudiobook and provide your e mail address in exchange for the free digital download. The audiobook will only be available on the website for a limited time as I offer free goodies to my readership on a regular basis.

Foreword by Lise Cartwright

Writing and self-publishing your own book seems so easy from the outset.

All you have to do is write your book, get it edited, formatted and then uploaded to Amazon... see, easy. Until you start the process that is.

I remember when I started down this path as a self-published author, I had plans to write 30 books within 12 months because I thought it would be soooooo simple and easy. Boy how wrong I was. (But I did manage to get 20 done!)

You'll often hear me saying to other indie authors, "The writing is the easy part!" and there's a reason that's the truth.

It wasn't until I learned things the hard way that I started to understand the process, a process that is not intuitive or easy to follow, but a process that, once understood and implemented, is rewarding on so many levels.

Imagine receiving a cardboard box in the mail, it's got no defining features about it except for a tiny Amazon logo on the shipping label. Your heart begins to race, could it be...? You rip open the box and inside is your first published book, in all it's paperback glory!

There is nothing that beats the feeling of seeing and holding your first book for the first time. It's almost like holding a newborn baby...

But I've skipped ahead too much! In order to achieve this, you have to start at the beginning and learn the process yourself.

This is where Paul's book comes in. As a beginner, you're probably already feeling overwhelmed with the writing part, now you're wondering how on earth you're going to get the book published let alone marketed and into the hands of your readers — you're hyperventilating and breaking out in cold sweats just thinking about it.

I understand and Paul does too. I've known Paul for just over 6 months now, and since he started his own self-publishing journey, he's had success after success with each new book.

The reason for this? He researched, questioned and implemented what he learned and then took his own book launch experiences and learned again and again.

He has walked the walk and now can talk the talk, because he's been there, understood how things worked and has had two successful bestselling book launches in a short period of time.

I've no doubt that you, the newbie author, will have no problem understanding what Paul has laid out for you in this book. By the end of it, you'll be your own little self- publishing superstar, able to boldly go where no newbie author has gone before!

I wish you all the best on your own self-publishing path and encourage you to read and reread Paul's book so that you understand the fundamentals involved in publishing and launching a bestselling book so you can experience this for yourself too.

To your success

Lise Cartwright - <u>Indie Author</u>
<u>www.authorbasics.com</u>

Foreword by Kevin Kruse

Would you like to make $100,000 or more as an author?

On January 1 of 2015 I quit my "day job" so I could become a full-time writer. My goal was to make a six figure income by the end of the year.

Knowing that it is difficult to make a full-time income just from book royalties (not impossible, just difficult) my plan was to spend most of my time writing and publishing my own books, but to use the books as a platform to other income streams including keynote speeches, workshops, and online training. I call this approach, being an "authorpreneur".

Knowing that the year would be filled with epic failures (lessons learned!) and hopefully some wins along the way, too, I decided to blog my entire journey at authorjourneyto100k.com. The good, the bad, the ugly on my march to $100,000.

To my complete and utter surprise, I broke the $100,000 barrier after only six months. And as I write this foreword now, in the middle of December, *I've already broken $200,000 for the year*.

As you can imagine, questions I'm frequently asked are, "How did you do it? How can *I* write and publish my own book?"

I'm fortunate in that I can now answer these questions in part by referring people to Paul Brodie's *Book Publishing For Beginners*. Paul offers very specific advice without the fluff, based on his own journey as an independent author. I've seen how Paul's momentum and success has grown with every new book he's released.

For example, getting book reviews is a notoriously difficult task and Paul is fully transparent when he shares that for his first book, *Eat Less and Move More*, only 12 people out of 100 he contacted actually left a book review. But Paul learned more effective tactics—fully detailed in Chapter 6—which enabled him to get 22 reviews for his second book, and 33 reviews for his third book.

Not everybody can become a $100,000 author; not everyone even *wants* to be a six figure author. But if you are looking to get in the indie publishing game, Book Publishing For Beginners can get you from first draft through a successful launch.

Kevin Kruse
Bucks County, PA
www.AuthorJourneyTo100K.com

Introduction

Welcome to Book Publishing for Beginners. This book will help you with launching your first (of hopefully many) book. My goal is to help you through the process of a completed manuscript to publishing your book and building your brand. I will also show you additional ways to increase your revenue streams through the sale of paperback books on createspace and audiobooks on audible.

Chapter 1: Editing your book – Starting with the expectation that you have completed at least a rough draft of your first manuscript. There are many great books out there that will help you with writing your book. The intention of this book is to help assist in taking your manuscript to a #1 bestselling book in your category.

Chapter 2: Having a great book cover design. (One of the most important parts of having a successful book launch) Having the right cover makes all the difference in a book that will sell and one that will not.

Chapter 3: How to create a book description - otherwise known as, sales copy. Your book description is just as important as having a great book cover design.

Chapter 4: Converting your book
- MOBI

Chapter 5: The uploading process to
category options for your book.

Chapter 6: How to get book reviews and
challenges involved. It is not an easy process
starting out and I will show you methods that I
have used to get reviews quickly.

Chapter 7: A case study introduction. I introduce
what will be covered in Chapters 8, 9, and 10 for
the case studies for my first three books.

Chapter 8: The first case study - I go through the
launch of my first book, Eat Less and Move More.
What worked well for the launch and what could
be improved.

Chapter 9: The second case study of the launch for
my second book, Motivation 101.

Chapter 10: Last case study of the launch for my
third book, Positivity Attracts.

Chapter 11: The ideal free launch strategy - I will
cover a launch strategy that can get you thousands
of downloads for $85.00.

Chapter 12: The ideal paid strategy at 99 cents. A
five day strategy to help you get anywhere from

sales prior to converting your price
. 9 cents to either $2.99 or $3.99.

Chapter 13: How to record an audiobook version of your book - Equipment needed to record it yourself and options to outsource the audiobook recording.

Chapter 14: The process to convert your book into paperback for createspace so that you can also have a paperback edition of your book to sell.

Chapter 15: How to build your email list

Chapter 16: Lead magnets and why they are critical to building your e mail list.

Chapter 17: A variety of different back end products that you can offer your readers.

Chapter 18: Different revenue streams that you can utilize as a Kindle author

I hope that this book helps you in your journey to become a bestselling author. It is a huge commitment to create and market a book. My wish is that this book will help you during your journey. My philosophy in anything I do from teaching, to giving motivational seminars, writing and coaching is to have the power of one. The power of one is my goal to help at least one person and I hope that person is you.

Coaching Offer

Are you looking for a coach to help with turning your book into a bestseller?

Are you looking for a coach to help with weight loss, increasing your motivation, or improving your positive thinking?

Contact Paul today at Brodie@BrodieEDU.com to set up a free call.

Check out www.brodieedu.com/coaching to see more information about Paul's coaching and how it can help you

Chapter 1 Editing Your Book

In July 2015, I wrote my first book Eat Less and Move More over three days. After my first draft was ready to go, I reached out to a friend of mine who is an excellent book editor. Her name is Devin Hacker and she has served as the editor for all of my books. Devin sliced and diced my first draft editing the grammatical errors, sentence fragments, and took out parts of chapters that did not flow.

I trusted Devin completely with this huge part of the process and ever since then our partnership has been wonderful. Having a great editor is critical and something I consider to be the most crucial part of finishing your book.

You can find very good editors on Fiverr.com or you can reach out to Devin as well. Editing can range anywhere from fifty dollars to several hundred dollars, so finding the right editor is very important.

After you have gone through your first and then final draft with your editor, I highly recommend one final process that I will cover later in this book. Uploading your book to Amazon and recording the audiobook version first and recording it yourself. This tends to be the best way to read a final proof. For my books, I have at least three people read it to catch errors, but no matter what, you will always find errors. That's part of being human. I found plenty of errors in all of my books. It's going to happen and the best way to catch those final errors is to read the book aloud yourself.

When you find the right editor, I recommend building a long term relationship with them. The more you work with the same person, the better the editing becomes as they get to know your writing style. Devin has done an incredible job with not only the edits, but also with keeping my tone and message.

Once the editing process is completed, it is then time to move on to getting your book cover.

**Download this guide on www.brodieedu.com/resources to see an example of my editing process and for the contact information for my own personal editor**

Chapter 2 Book Cover

The book cover is your window dressing. Choosing the right book cover is critical to your book becoming a successful, potentially #1 bestseller, or just another book. Covers can range in cost from several dollars to hundreds of dollars. As I had a small budget for my first book, Eat Less and Move More, I knew that I needed to get as much bang for the buck as possible.

I researched Fiverr extensively and found a freelancer who made book covers for a very inexpensive cost and had a great rating from customers. In fact, she has thousands of ratings so I figured I would give it a shot. I was not disappointed.

Everything on Fiverr is at least five dollars to start, but there are always extras. I chose the twenty dollar option for my first three books which included the five dollar gig, an additional five dollars for a high quality stock image, and ten dollars for the original psd file and pdf. This was a great investment so I could have the master copy in case I ever needed to make any changes.

In my request for my first book cover, I asked for a blue and black color scheme. Within four days

Vikiana delivered my first book cover and I loved it.

I have the image of the book cover on the next page.

I knew similarly to Devin, that I found a long term partner for my books. Vikiana has made all of my book covers and she has done an incredible job for an amazing low price.

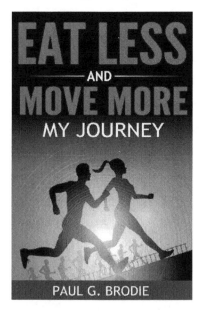

Download this guide on www.brodieedu.com/resources to see an example of all my book covers and to get the contact information for my designer

Chapter 3 Book Description is Your Sales Copy

Sales copy is what will help sell your book. The goal of sales copy should be to help the reader identify a problem that you will help solve. There is a great article from New York Times Bestselling Author, Kevin Kruse, which explains how to write sales copy that I highly recommend - you can check it out here. I came upon this resource while my third book, Positivity Attracts was getting ready to launch.

For my first book, Eat Less and Move More, I researched many top authors and looked at their styles. After looking at many book descriptions, I came up with the following for Eat Less and Move More.

Eat Less and Move More: My Journey shows you how you can **change your lifestyle** *without spending long hours in the gym and without starving yourself while enjoying cheat meals.*

On May 2, 2011, I received my wake up call. I was 336 pounds, had borderline type 2 diabetes, and was recently recovered from both bronchitis and pneumonia. My bad eating habits and lifestyle choices were making me ill, but I was too wrapped up in what I was doing to spot the signs let alone to do anything about it. **That day I found myself in the doctor's office and was told that I might not be around in 5-10 years if I didn't change my lifestyle.** That was my wake-up call. Luckily I got a second chance.

That day I realized that <u>life is short and precious</u> and I made a decision that I was going to do things differently. I decided to change my life so that I could **live life to the fullest** and **eat less and move more**.

What I decided to create for myself was:

• A healthy lifestyle that **I could be proud of**
• The **mental freedom** to live the life of my dreams
• The **freedom of good health** to do the things I love and to be with the people who matter most to me

And now I want to help you do the same.

After all, deciding to start your journey to **eat less and move more** is something you do because you have a vision of a better life for you and your family. **It's your chance to take control and live life on your terms**. And done right *<u>it will give you</u> the mental freedom and the freedom of good health to do the things you love, when you want to do them and <u>with</u> the people who matter most in your life.*

Eat Less and Move More will show you how to create an improved you that gives you the time to work on your own passions in life. It will also show you the mistakes that I made and what I did when I gained over half of the weight back. I also tell my story throughout the book of working in the corporate world and eventually leaving that world to pursue a career in teaching as my weight and career were connected.

In short, losing weight and keeping the weight off is not a temporary change but a lifestyle choice by choosing to **eat less and move more.**

Eat Less and Move More shows you how you can easily start your own **journey towards a healthier lifestyle** – a lifestyle that you can be proud of *and* achieve both ***mental freedom*** and ***freedom of good health.***

But more than this, Eat Less and Move More explores what it means to live a truly happy and fulfilled life – to *really live the life of your dreams and pursue what you love.* It encourages you to examine your own motivations and desires in order to **determine your path in life.**

To get access to the bonus materials and resources (all for FREE), be sure to visit:

www.BrodieEDU.com

It was not bad for my first launch, but after reading Kevin's article, I changed my approach for sales copy and created the following sales copy for Eat Less and Move More. I made these changes in late November. One of the best things about Kindle is that you can change and update your book and change your book description whenever you want to.

Here is the new and improved sales copy.

Eat Less and Move More: My Journey shows how you can **change your mindset** and **improve your physical and mental health**.

What if a few new habits could improve your personal health? What if you could increase your health and happiness with a few simple steps? Imagine waking up in the morning feeling healthy and happy and ready to take on the day.

Amazon bestselling author, Paul G. Brodie, in his first book, covers multiple ways to improve your physical and mental health.

Here are a few things that you will get out of Eat Less and Move More.

In this book, you will learn.

• How to learn to Listen to Your Body
• How to take a Leap of Faith and Follow Your Dreams
• How to respond when your body gives you a Wakeup Call
• How to Eat Less and Move More
• How to respond if you gain weight after an initial weight loss
• How to create a healthy environment by Eating Clean
• How to Change Your Lifestyle at any age

• How to utilize Healthy Eating Habits in your everyday life

• How to enjoy Cheat Meals without feeling guilty

• BONUS: Daily Food Lists for what Paul has utilized to lose over sixty pounds and current food items that he eats to continue to live a healthy lifestyle

Buy this book NOW to increase your personal physical and mental health

Pick up your copy today by clicking the BUY NOW button at the top of this page!

To get access to the bonus materials and resources (all for FREE), be sure to visit:

www.BrodieEDU.com

As you can see, I made a much better effort in identifying a problem for the reader and offering solutions. In addition, I added two calls to action at the end of the sales copy by telling the reader to buy now. Calls to action may sound basic, but they do work.

Once you have completed your sales copy you will need to have it converted to html. I found a freelancer on Fiverr called Kindleserge who converts my sales copy for five dollars. Once you get the file back it will be in a txt file. I have utilized Kindleserge for my first three launches. Recently I have learned more about html and created the html update for the book description for both Eat Less and Move More and Motivation 101 during the Thanksgiving break. Both descriptions look great and from now on I will be updating the books in html myself.

At this point you will want to go to Amazon and to Author Central. In Author Central you can add your personal information with an Author bio and pictures. When you are ready to upload your book you will have the option to add your sales copy in the book description. With the html code, the sales copy will pop and you will have the ability to bold words in order to help grab the reader's attention. The sales copy should also be used in the back of your paperback book, which we will cover later.

__Download this guide on www.brodieedu.com/resources to see additional examples of sales copy for all my books and for an html guide for your own book description__

Chapter 4 Converting Your Book to Kindle

You will need to convert your book to MOBI format. Fiverr has many freelancers who will convert your word file to MOBI. It will typically cost between twenty five and fifty dollars for the conversion. You can also do it yourself with a program called Scrivener. I have not used it because I prefer to have it converted to Kindle as many things can go wrong with MOBI conversions. The freelancer I use is gigsterready and she typically takes three to four days to complete the conversion, but she does great work. Eat Less and Move More was over eighteen thousand words and cost fifty dollars. Both Motivation 101 and Positivity Attracts were thirty dollars each for the conversion as both books were a little over nine thousand words.

Chapter 5 Uploading Your Book and Kindle Direct Publishing

I strongly recommend uploading your book one week prior to your official launch. I did this for my first launch with Eat Less and Move More. Initially, I thought that I should have waited two weeks in order to submit the book to many of the free ebook sites that are available to help promote your book. Most of those sites require two weeks advanced notice but I did not find that many of the free sites would promote the book. After my third launch for Positivity Attracts, I found that I was able to still get the main book sites for my promotions and also maximize the time for when it would be on the bestseller list as a hot new release, which I will cover later in this book.

To upload your book to Amazon you will need the MOBI file, the book cover, and your sales copy to add to the book description. The instructions are pretty simple to follow on Amazon for this process as long as you have those three files.

When you are uploading your book, you will have the option to sign up for Kindle Direct Publishing (KDP) Select. Taking advantage of this will help with your launch and it allows you to choose one of two promotions. The only drawback is that your ebook will be exclusive to Amazon for 90 days. You can then take your ebook out of KDP after the 90 day period if you choose to.

I kept my first book, Eat Less and Move More in KDP for an additional three months. In the future I will be making some changes as to how I execute this which I discuss in the first chapter of my next book, Book Publishing for Authors (chapter 1 is available here as a free download).

In KDP Select, you can choose either five free days for your promo (which I suggest) or you can have a Kindle countdown where you can sell your book for 99 cents for seven days and still get your 70 percent royalty. Usually, when your book is under $2.99 your book will only be eligible for a 35 percent royalty. With the Kindle countdown, you get 70 cents instead of 35 cents at the 99 cent price point.

I suggest choosing the five day free promo, but we will get to that later on in the book. The goal in my view, especially as a new author, is to get your book into as many hands as possible. The best way to do that is to utilize the free promotion so you have the potential to get your books to thousands of readers and those readers can purchase your future books, sign up for your e mail list, and purchase back end products including coaching, courses, etc.

By signing up in KDP select, you will also be enrolled in the KDP Select Global Fund. The fund is for both Kindle Unlimited and the Kindle Owners Lending Library. You get paid for each page a potential customer reads of your book.

The Kindle Unlimited program is essentially Netflix for Amazon Kindle where for a flat fee, the reader gets unlimited Kindle books to read. You do get a percentage of revenue based on how many pages (called Kindle Edition Normalized Pages/KNEP) are read. It is not a huge amount but over time, with a lot of pages read, it can add up. You do have the option to sign up for the Kindle Owners Lending Library where readers that buy your book can lend the Kindle book to a friend or family member. Again, the goal is to get as many people to read your ebook as possible so I definitely recommend signing up for the Kindle book lending option.

Another great resource is the Kindle MatchBook. The Kindle MatchBook option gives readers who bought the paperback edition of your book the option to purchase the Kindle version for either 99 cents or free. I go with the 99 cents option because since the reader has already bought your paperback edition, they will most likely take advantage of the discount and it will count as a sale.

Next comes choosing your sales categories. You are responsible for designating two categories to your book. It is CRUCIAL to have your book in two different categories if you want to be as successful as possible. Furthermore, where you place your book is extremely critical too. For my books I looked at two main categories with Business & Money and Biographies & Memoirs. Both main categories are ones that sell very well. I also wanted to get into as many sub categories in those areas as possible.

For example, in Motivation 101 I placed the book into the following category. Kindle Store>Kindle eBooks>Business & Money>Economics>Urban & Regional. I chose the main category as Business & Money, then dug deeper to find deeper categories inside Business & Money. In Urban & Regional I found a deep category to place my book that was not highly competitive. Motivation 101 was #1 in that category almost every day since launching. It also will show up in multiple categories with finding a deeper category. For example

Motivation 101 was #1 in Urban & Regional and also in the top books in Economics and also in Business & Money. Your book and rating are shown in many categories, which help to increase traffic to your book. This is especially beneficial during your launch as your book will be showing up in the hot new releases section of all of those categories.

I typically choose a category that is not highly competitive for the first category and then find a tougher category for the second. For overall ranking, look for the top three books in the categories that are ranked from 5000-10000 overall in Amazon Kindle. Those are great categories to potentially place your books. With Motivation 101 I put the book in the following second category Kindle Store>Kindle eBooks>Nonfiction>Self-Help>Creativity. There are many categories to look at and it's important to find a category that has the top ranked books ranked around 10,000 to 20,000 in Amazon Kindle. Having your book as the top ranked book in your category also gives you that great orange sticker from Amazon that says Amazon #1 bestseller in that category. Potential readers are typically impressed when a book shows that it is a best seller.

Once you upload your book you will need to set a price. As I mentioned, I set my price at 99 cents. The drawback is that it is only a 35 percent royalty versus 70 percent for $2.99. However, each unit on Amazon counts as a unit sold regardless of the price. Having the price at 99 cents will help boost early sales and also with getting reviews prior to the official book launch.

__Download this guide on www.brodieedu.com/resources to see a step-by-step guide to upload your book to Amazon__

Chapter 6 Getting Reviews

This is one of the toughest things to do as an author. For your first launch I would suggest reaching out to friends, family, acquaintances, and Facebook friends to get honest reviews. I ended up contacting over 100 people for my first book launch. Out of those 100 people contacted, only 12 people submitted reviews. The good part is that once you get to know fellow authors in Facebook groups then you are eventually able to build upon your brand and you will get more reviews. This has proven as Eat Less and Move more has 17 reviews, Motivation 101 has 22 reviews and Positivity Attracts after only a few weeks on Amazon has 33 reviews.

For your first book through the process will be tough. People you think you can rely on will most likely let you down. One of the things I would recommend is to do the strategy that I did for my third book, Positivity Attracts.

One strategy I found to be helpful was uploading the final version of the pdf file to Dropbox and then sending the link to fellow author pals and a few friends that are always helpful and leave reviews for me on both Amazon and Goodreads. You will definitely want reviews on both pages as

Goodreads readers can be very critical about books. They are very passionate and tend to consider very good books to be only 3 to 4 stars while Amazon readers will typically grade your book as 4 to 5 stars.

Be sure to send follow up messages to your potential reviewers too. I would recommend sending out the advance copies a week before you upload your book to Amazon. Once you upload to Amazon send a follow up message to ask if they had a chance to read the book. Let them know that the book is uploaded and is available for 99 cents and that you could really use their support by downloading a copy and leaving you a review.

I have found this to work pretty well but I would not recommend contacting the same person more than two times.

Another tactic that you can do is creating a book launch group on Facebook. You can invite your Facebook friends to the group and post regularly in the group. I had a Facebook group for my third launch and would say that I have fifteen reviews in my launch group, which was awesome.

Download this guide on www.brodieedu.com/resources to see message examples that I have used to reach out to friends, family and fellow authors for reviews

Chapter 7 Case Study Intro

There are several ways to launch a book. Over the next three chapters, I will share what I have utilized to generate over 2900 free downloads for my first two books, Eat Less and Move More and Motivation 101 and over 4500 downloads for Positivity Attracts. Both Motivation 101 and Positivity Attracts have become Amazon bestsellers. I will also share all of the details of my third launch for Positivity Attracts where I spent a total of $85.00 on advertising during the free launch and ended up with over 4500 downloads and the book peaked at #79 in all of Amazon Kindle.

My strategy is to have a free launch for 3.5 to 4.5 days. This strategy generates a lot of positive publicity and helps with my philosophy of getting the book into as any hands as possible. As I have several back end products, including both motivational speaking and coaching as my goal is maximum exposure for the back end.

__Download this guide on www.brodieedu.com/resources to see additional examples of back end products that you can add in your books__

Chapter 8 Case Study for Eat Less and Move More

I launched my first book on Sunday, August 9, 2015. One week prior to the launch I posted a video on Facebook and on my amazon author page to promote the first book. I also posted a second video on the weekend of the free launch prior to leaving to Chicago for a conference I would be at for that week.

On Day #1, I promoted the book through several methods. The first was posting the book link and a message about the book on my personal Facebook page.

Here was the message.

Greetings from Chicago! I am proud to announce that my first eBook has officially launched on Amazon and is FREE for the next several days. Please help support the book launch by downloading the eBook on Amazon today. This book is deeply personal to me as it is an open, honest, and fairly blunt look at the journey of personal transformation and how it has changed my life for the better. It also details my struggles to keep the weight off and what I have done on the path to Eat Less and Move More. I sincerely hope that you enjoy reading my first eBook.

Book Link was also included in the message

I used a very similar message to post in over 50 Facebook Kindle groups. Things have changed recently though and I would suggest being really careful about posting in Facebook Kindle groups as several posts have gotten reported for being posted too much. Last thing you want to do is end up in Facebook jail as they will put you in timeout (no Facebook access) for 1-2 weeks and also remove every post that you have ever posted in a group. For my third launch I only posted on my personal page and author page. I also posted updates to how the book was doing in a few author Facebook groups but that was all I would post.

I also had twenty people share my book on their personal Facebook pages. After the end of day #1 I had 308 downloads. Day #2 would prove to be a huge day.

On Monday, August 10, I scheduled a Freebooksy promotion for day #2 and it was huge. At the end of day #2 I had 1619 downloads and was #1 in my categories and also entered the top 100 in Amazon Kindle overall with a peak rank of #94. Freebooksy costs $80.00 and is well worth the investment. I posted several status updates on Facebook to keep the positive momentum going.

On Tuesday, August 12, we had 776 downloads by the end of day #3. On Wednesday, August 13, we had 210 downloads for day #4 and I ended the free promotion at 3:00 pm that day and switched to paid. My launch strategy was to have the price at 99 cents for a couple weeks and then raise the price to $2.99.

We had 2913 downloads for the launch of my first book and I was thrilled. The book sold well for the next several weeks. My biggest mistake was not raising the price until the end of August. I also did not have any paid promotions for the book except for a few on Fiverr, which did not work out well. The book sold well at 99 cents, but sales plummeted when I raised the price to $2.99.

What that meant was that I was making 35 cents per book primarily instead of over two dollars, which is the price point to actually make a decent amount of money on your book. I researched several paid promotions and would be ready for the launch of book #2, Motivation 101.

Chapter 9 Case Study for Motivation 101

After learning my lesson for the mistakes with Eat Less and Move More, I had a much better game plan for Motivation 101. Only problem was that I did not like the cover. Originally I gave away around 100 copies of the book as a PDF when I was at a national leadership conference and convention in Chicago. I was giving my Motivation 101 seminar (the book was created from the seminar) in Chicago and wanted to give my attendees a sneak preview. Here was the original cover.

The cover just did not work. I asked both my editor and several friends and family for their thoughts and they suggested that I should change the cover if I was unhappy with it. I reached out to my designer and told her that I wanted to change the design and started a new order. I made it clear that I wanted a sunset or sunrise and wanted Motivation 101 to look very bold in the title. This is what she designed for me.

I loved the new cover and it was definitely the right decision.

On Sunday, October 4, I launched Motivation 101. I uploaded the book on September 18. I did this as I have heard through several Facebook groups that were created specifically for authors that it is best to upload your books at least two weeks prior as many of the free newsletter promotions will not accept your book. The goal during free launches is to get the book into as many hands as possible so I decided to try this tactic. To save time I bought a $14.99 free book promotion tool from Book Marketing Tools. The tool was easy to use but I was not happy with it as I was only featured on two promotional sites. One was on freebooksforme and the other was on ebookdaily. Prior to the launch I posted a video on Facebook to promote the first book

I used a similar tactic for Eat Less and Move More and started with a status update on Facebook and posted in 75 Facebook Kindle groups. Again, this was before Facebook started to police the Kindle groups so this is a tactic that I caution you to be careful with. Day #1 ended with 318 units through social media posts. This was ten more downloads than the first launch and my only goal for the launch was to end up with more downloads than Eat Less and Move More.

Monday, October 5, was the Freebooksy promotion and ended up with 1610 downloads and made it to the top 100 again in Amazon

Kindle with a ranking of #97. After day #2 we were virtually even with the first launch. Tuesday, October 6, had 776 downloads for day #3 and Wednesday, October 7, and 296 downloads for a total of 2945 downloads. The goal to have a bigger launch than the first book was a success with having 26 more downloads. I used the same marketing strategies for the first book and posted status updates on Monday and Wednesday about how well the book was doing. Now it was time to make some money!

I was finally able to get a Buck Books promotion. They don't always have openings but I was able to get a promotion for Sunday, October 11, and it was huge! I was also able to get a promotion for Eat Less and Move More for the same day. It was well worth it as I sold 102 copies of Motivation 101 during the promotion and 59 copies of Eat Less and Move More. I reached out to an author pal (Mark L. Messick) on Tuesday and asked for his advice. Motivation was #1 in all of its categories and was in the top 2259 paid in all of Amazon Kindle. He suggested that I immediately raise the price on both books to $2.99 so that I could go from making 34 cents a book to over two dollars. I agreed to take the leap of faith.

He told me that the book sales might plummet for a couple of days but that the book would rebound once the Amazon Algorithm kicks in. The Amazon Algorithm, while a little complicated to explain basically helps when a new book is out and is doing well. As Amazon also wants books to do well and make money they will recommend books that sell well in a category in other books called Customers Who Bought This Item Also Bought.

My sales did drop after the first full day of raising the price to one sale. After that second day I averaged double digit sales for several weeks and it was well worth taking the risk. I made over $400.00 for the month and a lot of that revenue was due to what Mark suggested.

I found that most authors do not make much starting out but I was averaging at least a hundred and fifty dollars per month and what I have made has increased each month. For December my goal is to make one thousand dollars and we are on pace to do so.

Motivation 101 has sold well since the launch and paid promotion with Buck Books. I also purchased a promotion with Awesome Gang for November 1. It only cost me ten dollars. I reduced the price of the book to 99 cents for a few days to boost the sales ranking and it worked well. I had 8-10 sales for three days straight before raising the price back to $2.99.

One thing I have learned is that you must constantly find ways to promote your book and drive traffic to your book site. By lowering the price for a couple of days a month and dropping the price, it can really help boost your book rankings.

Motivation 101 has been #1 in its main category since it launched. I was able to find a great category in Business & Investing in a subcategory that was not highly competitive. Currently both Motivation 101 and Positivity Attracts have held the #1 ranking in their categories since transitioning from free to paid.

Chapter 10 Case Study for Positivity Attracts

The launch for Positivity Attracts was huge and we got a total of 4519 free downloads during the launch. The cover was awesome and I did not need to make any changes.

I uploaded the book on Saturday, November 14. For whatever reason, Amazon listed November 13 as the publication date, but that's no big deal. I went against conventional wisdom and did not upload it two weeks prior. The reason that I didn't is that I noticed a slight decrease in sales for my previous book, Motivation 101 after one month. I want to keep Positivity Attracts in the hot new releases section for as long as possible while it is in the paid category. With this strategy, I will have more time to maximize the sales potential.

I reached out to fifteen different ebook promotion companies and submitted a free non-guaranteed promotion for each company. I also made sure that I had at least five reviews before submitting the book as many of those companies require at least five reviews to be considered. For my previous book, I used the $14.99 free book promotion tool from Book Marketing Tools and I did not feel it was worth it.

The only paid promotions I used for this launch were BKnights on Fiverr (well worth it) and Freebooksy $80.00 (worth at least 2500 downloads on this launch overall). With BKnights I bought both the $5.00 promotion and the $5.00 add on to be featured in their daily newsletter. I found out during this launch that the daily newsletter promotion is only a link to their website and the newsletter add on is not worth getting. I would suggest sticking to the basic $5.00 promotion as it is a great value.

Sunday, November 22 (728 downloads). BKnights promotion and the book was also featured for free in Free99Books and eBookStage. Ended Day #1 ranked 326 overall in Amazon Kindle.

Monday, November 23 (1850 downloads). Freebooksy promotion. I have used Freebooksy for all three of my book launches and the promotion has averaged at least 2000 downloads for each book. Ended Day #2 breaking into the top 100 overall, and ranked #95. I posted a status update on my Facebook personal and author pages and in several awesome author Facebook groups.

Tuesday November 24 (792 downloads) Peaked at #79 overall and stayed in the top 100 until the evening and ended the day ranked #110 overall. I posted a status update on my Facebook personal and author pages.

Wednesday, November 25 (631 downloads) BKnights ran the promotion again for me as I reached out to them about a couple of questions I had about their listing process and e mail. Started the day at #130 and ended the day at #138.

Thursday, November 26 (518 downloads) No promotions on Thursday. Started the day at #136 and ended the promotion at #144.

The book was #1 in its categories for the entire promotion.

I switched to paid at 6:30 pm central time on Thanksgiving and had 14 sales that evening. On Friday November 27 I had 35 sales. This is at the 99 cent price point. Saturday November 28 I had 44 sales and had a promotion through Reading Deals.

On Sunday, I had a Books Butterfly promotion with 53 sales. Monday was the promotion with Buck Books on also Bookzio. Between those two promotions I had 92 sales which took the book to the top 1357 in all of Amazon.

Positivity Attracts was #1 in all three paid categories and ranked 1357 at its highest ranking during the 99 cent price point.

On Tuesday, December 1, I changed the price from 99 cents to $2.99 at noon Central Time. I had 18 sales with no promotions that morning. After I converted the book to 2.99 I had an additional 11 sales the rest of the day that took my profit margin from 35 cents to $2.06 per book sold. Wednesday had 19 sales and Thursday and Friday had 10 sales.

Overall, I was really pleased with the launch as I am averaging at least 40 dollars a day in passive income. Having the book for an additional week in the hot new releases is also increasing exposure and creating more traffic to the book.

One of the most important equations I have learned was thanks to fellow author, Mark L. Messick. He told me that traffic plus conversion equals sales. You want to drive as much traffic as possible to your book site on Amazon through marketing your book as much as possible during the launch phases. You get the conversion from your book cover and book description/sales copy. In the next chapter I will cover the ideal way to launch your book while it is free.

Chapter 11 Free Launch Strategy

In the case study chapters I have covered a few different ways to launch your book. I am going to give you a marketing plan to promote your book that I feel will be a great potential way for you to launch your book. This strategy will cost you $85.00 for your non-fiction book.

What I first suggest is to decide whether you want to do a four or five day strategy for your free launch. Again, as an author who is starting out I would definitely suggest going the free route to get your book into as many hands as possible. In chapter 16 I will cover potential lead magnets that you may want to consider should you want to build an e mail list of potential customers to sell your products to (highly recommend going this route).

After deciding whether you want to go the four or five day route you will want to decide on dates. My launches always start on Sunday. On Sunday morning I create a status update on Facebook about my book being free to encourage people to check it out while free. I also post it in several Facebook author groups. What I no longer suggest doing is posting it in a lot of Kindle Facebook groups. However, I do have a list of a few Kindle

Facebook groups that you might want to consider posting your book in.

Here is what I typically post in the Kindle Facebook groups.

FREE on Amazon Kindle today October 4 until October 7! *FREE* with Kindle Unlimited!

Motivation 101 shows you how you can easily start your own journey towards a healthier mindset – a mindset that you can be proud of _and_ *achieve mental freedom.*

But more than this, Motivation 101 explores what it means to live a truly happy and fulfilled life – to *really live the life of your dreams and pursue what you love.* It encourages you to examine your own motivations and desires in order to determine your path in life.

http://www.amazon.com/Motivation-101-Increase-Brodie-Seminar-ebook/dp/B015LEKE6O/ref=sr_1_1?ie=UTF8&qid=1443659794&sr=8-1&keywords=motivation+101

I also posted in the comment section about my audiobook that I was giving away as a lead magnet during that launch.

Free audiobook for Motivation 101 is available at www.BrodieEDU.com/freeaudiobook

I used this strategy for my first two book launches and it should generate at least 50-100 free downloads. I have provided a link at the end of this chapter to a free resource that I am giving away with those Kindle Facebook groups that I have seen still used by fellow authors. Again, I do not use them but if you are interested then I invite you to check them out.

Here is an example of what I am now doing for all of my book launches going forward.

Sunday Day #1. BKnights Promotion (costs $5.00 on Fiverr.com), Facebook status update and posting in author Facebook pages (Pats' First Kindle Group, Author Basics, Authority Self-Publishing). Submit the book for a potential free listing with Free99Books and eBookStage. This process brought me 728 downloads on my last launch.

Monday Day #2. Freebooksy Promotion (costs $80.00 on freebooksy.com). This is the best investment that you can make in my view for your free launch. This brought me 1850 downloads on day #2 of my last launch. I will typically post a status update on this day about the launch on my personal Facebook and author page showing how well the book launch is going. This will be the day that your book is most likely at its highest rank.

Positivity Attracts was up to #83 in all of Amazon Kindle at this point.

Tuesday Day #3. No promotions. Had 792 downloads on my last launch for Positivity Attracts. Typically there are readers from Freebooksy that might not check their e mail right away and I have always had a second day of strong downloads from Freebooksy readers. Most of the downloads will be in the morning. Positivity Attracts actually peaked at #79 in all of Amazon Kindle during Tuesday morning of day #3.

Wednesday Day #4. No promotions. However, I was a little concerned about BKnights as I had trouble finding my book on their website. I contacted them on Tuesday and they offered to give me a refund if I was not happy with their service. Instead, I told them I was pleased with the results but did ask them to post the book again on their website and they agreed. On Wednesday Day #4 I ended the day with 631 downloads.

Thursday Day #5 was the day that I decided to end the promotion at 6:30 pm central time. This would have the book available in prime time (7:00 to 11:00 pm) on Amazon and I wanted to have the book converted to paid as soon to prime time as possible.

After converting it to paid it still would show up in the free rankings for a couple of hours. The book would show a 99 cent price point and it should generate sales for your book. After the conversion Positivity Attracts was #1 in all three book categories and was in the top 2400 in all of Amazon Kindle.

As you have seen in my case studies, I have tried several different methods for when the book is launching for free. Each of my launches has done very well with my last launch doing record numbers.

With the launches I want to generate as much buzz as possible and having your book for free for a limited time definitely helps in that process. In chapter 16 we will cover lead magnets and how you can build your e mail list. Once you have several thousand people on your list then I would suggest considering not having a free launch as you will already have a strong list of people that will be interested in buying what you are offering not only with your book but also print and audiobooks.

In addition, hopefully you will have additional products that you will offer down the line with webinars, coaching, public speaking, and courses on Udemy.

__Download this guide on www.brodieedu.com/resources to see links for the Facebook Kindle groups to potentially promote your book__

Chapter 12 Paid Strategy at 99 Cents

Now that you have converted your book to 99 cents it is time to generate traffic to your book and get as many sales as possible. I am following similar concepts from the free strategy with having the book at 99 cents for the next 4.5 days. This is what I use.

Thursday evening. Convert your book around 6:30 pm central time. For Positivity Attracts we had 14 sales that evening and the book was in the top 2400 in all of Amazon Kindle and #1 in all three of its categories.

Day #1 Friday. No promotions and had 35 sales. Amazon will see your book doing well and it will start to be shown in the Customers Who Bought This Item Also Bought section of Kindle Books on Amazon. This is great publicity for your book and should help bring in sales.

Day #2 Saturday. Reading Deals promotion. They have 15,000 readers and it only costs $15.00. On day #2 I had 44 sales for Positivity Attracts.

Day #3 Sunday. Books Bufferfly promotion. The promotion I got was the $25.00 silver promotion. I had 53 sales for Positivity Attracts.

Day #4 Monday. Buck Books promotion ($35.00). I LOVE Buck Books. They have a great promotional strategy displaying both non-fiction and fiction ebooks in their daily e mail. They only show the links and typically have a great (and usually very funny) description for each book that makes the reader interested in clicking the link.

I also had a promotion with BookZio that I paid $29.00 for. The Grande option costs $19.99 and they have an option for pay an additional $10.00 for have your book listed as the first one in their daily e mail that I highly recommend. BookZio features a lot of books in their daily e mail and you definitely want to consider investing $10.00 in having your book be the first one that readers see when opening their e mail. I had 92 sales for Positivity Attracts that day thanks to both promotions and the book peaked at 1357 in all of Amazon Kindle and #1 in all three categories.

Day #5 Tuesday. No promotions. Convert your price from 99 cents to either $2.99 or $3.99 at noon central time. Mark mentioned that $3.99 is a great price point if your book is over 70 pages. I agree with his assessment.

My price was set to $2.99 as Positivity Attracts was under 70 pages. Sales will slip but remember that your book will be making $2.06 cents per sale instead of .35 cents. Do not worry if things slow down for a day or two. The Amazon Algorithm will kick in and you should see your books getting featured in the Customers Also Bought section of many top books. I saw this for both Motivation 101 and Positivity Attracts daily. I checked the Buck Books daily email for the next several days and I saw my books getting featured in the Customers Also Bought section every day.

The books that get promoted on Buck Books usually end up in the top 8000 at minimum in Amazon Kindle and I have seen quite a few in the top 2000. You will most likely see your book in that section so definitely subscribe to Buck Books for their daily e mail as it is an efficient way to track your book in that section.

Chapter 13 Recording Your Audiobook

Multiple revenue streams are critical to becoming not only a successful author, but also in any business. I recently read an article that explained the average millionaire entrepreneur had an average of seven revenue streams. Audiobooks are another great revenue stream to have as an author.

I decided to add audiobooks to my launches starting with my second book, Motivation 101. With my first book, Eat Less and Move More, I was incredibly busy with the launch and I did not have time to get the audiobook done at the time of the launch. After the launch finished I started to research audiobook options and found that I could do it myself.

I bought a condenser microphone called the Blue Snowball ICE Condenser Microphone and a pop filter from Amazon. The cost was around $56.00 for both and I downloaded the Audacity program for free, which would allow me to record the book. You will also need to reach out to your freelancer and have them convert your Kindle book cover to audiobook size. It shouldn't cost too much and having the cover is just as important for sales as it is for a Kindle cover. Unfortunately, I found this out the hard way. I did not have audiobook covers ready for several weeks after both Motivation 101 and Eat Less and Move More audiobooks were published. This was a mistake I do not plan to repeat as it did cost me revenue.

For Motivation 101, I wanted to have an Audiobook available at the time of the launch for two reasons. The first was to have the additional revenue stream and the second was to use it as a lead magnet.

I recorded the book over two weekends. There is a lot of work that goes into recording it yourself, so you need to decide if you want to take on that responsibility or work a royalty agreement out with having someone else record it for you. I have gone both routes.

Over the two weekends Motivation 101 was recorded, it took me two to three hours each weekend to record the audio. It was not an easy process, but I did learn a few things that I will cover.

My first suggestion is to record the smaller chapters first. This also includes the intro, foreword (if you have one), contact information, and some of the smaller chapters. Leave the longer chapters for the following weekend. You will make mistakes and you will have to rerecord chapters again. It is a frustrating process at times, but it does get better.

When I recorded Positivity Attracts, it was much easier and took me four hours instead of five to six hours. I do HIGHLY recommend finding a small room to record in. Do not have the air conditioning or heating on, you want the room as quiet as possible. I also recommend having the mic on at least three to four large hardback books and have the mic six inches from your face. This will help in case your computer fan is a little loud. You will want to speak into the mic at all times.

Once you have recorded a chapter I highly recommend that you listen to it immediately. If it sounds good and you are happy with it, go to the next chapter. Continue the process for those two weekends until your audiobook is complete. I also recommend taking a 5-10 minute break each hour. You will want to get some water and possibly some hot tea as your vocal chords will get tired. In addition, when recording, you will also want to pause before speaking at the start of each chapter for 2-3 seconds and then start to speak. At the end of each chapter also leave 2-3 seconds of silence.

Once your recording is complete, you will want to send the files to someone who can edit and remaster your recording. In audiobook recordings, ACX wants there to be a slight gap at the beginning and end of each chapter. The 2-3 seconds of silence is that gap. Your freelancer can make this flow very smoothly, but you do need to leave that space.

I have utilized fellow author Derek Doepker to remaster my audiobooks. He charges 25-50 dollars to remaster your audio and is well worth the investment. Derek will charge a higher rate if there are major things to fix if there are a lot of pops and clicks in your recording so please be aware of that.

I also employ another freelancer from Fiverr due to some problems with the audiobook recording of Positivity Attracts. Unfortunately, ACX is not always consistent with approving audiobooks. Sometimes they will approve it immediately, which they did for Motivation 101.

With Positivity Attracts, they rejected it as they heard too many pops and clicks. Uploading to ACX is a gamble because you might get an audio engineer who is not very picky or you may one who is extremely picky. I knew Positivity Attracts was a much better audiobook recording, but that is the luck of the draw.

I knew that with Derek, the cost would be significant because he would have to go through over an hour of the recording to fix it, so I found another freelancer. For $38.00 he went back and took out each pop and click. I got the files back and uploaded them again to ACX and it was approved within a few days. At the end of this chapter I am offering a free audiobook guide including Derek's contact information and also the link for my freelancer on Fiverr.

Once your audio is remastered and edited you will need to get an account set up on ACX.com when you are ready to upload should you record it yourself. They will give you several options for royalties.

For Motivation 101, I chose the 25 percent option. The 25 percent royalty option gave me rights to have my audiobook on my own website and I could also sell it separately. Since the Motivation 101 audiobook was also going to be my lead magnet, I was alright with losing a little money long term to get more readers funneled to my list. I could have chosen the 40 percent option, but that would have made the Motivation 101 audiobook exclusive to ACX.

With Positivity Attracts, I chose the 40 percent option. My strategy is to always think long-term. This business is a long term investment and I felt comfortable having the Motivation 101 audiobook as the only audiobook magnet that I would offer.

For my first book, Eat Less and Move More, I decided that I did not want to record it myself. My other books were around 10,000 words and Eat Less and Move More was almost twice as long. I chose to do a royalty share agreement and had a narrator on ACX do the recording. This option only gives you 20 percent commission as the narrator also gets 20 percent as well. Since I did not want to record it, I felt that 20 percent of something was better than 20 percent of nothing.

It is an easy process as you submit the information on ACX and narrators will audition for you. After listening to ten auditions, I chose my narrator and he recorded the book within five days. The narrator also uploads the audiobook to ACX, which is great. It was available on Amazon, Audible, and iTunes within two weeks.

One other thing about ACX is that the audiobook will most likely not be ready in time for your launch. You cannot upload the audiobook until your Kindle ebook is available on Amazon. At that point you can upload the book. Again, the audiobooks are a long-term investment. You will not make a ton of money starting out and might only make 10-20 dollars for the first couple of months. It should pay off long term.

Another great benefit of recording it yourself is that you find errors in your book that you may not have caught initially. No matter how awesome your editor is (and I have an AMAZING editor) there will be mistakes that do not get caught. Recording the audiobook out loud will help you find the other mistakes. I have found at least ten errors with both Motivation 101 and Positivity Attracts while recording the audiobooks.

If you are going to record an audiobook yourself, I would recommend recording the audiobook first before having your book converted to Kindle. For Positivity Attracts I used the Microsoft Word version of my book to record the audiobooks and then made corrections to any errors found to the file while recording the audiobook, I had it converted to Kindle and then paperback. I will be covering the paperback process in our next chapter.

Download this free audiobook guide on www.brodieedu.com/resources to see the process to record your audiobook and for the contact information for my freelancers

Chapter 14 Converting Your Book to Paperback

Once you have recorded your audiobook and corrected any final errors to your book (most likely in a Microsoft Word file) to send to your freelancer for Kindle MOBI conversion then it is time to convert your book to paperback.

Converting your word file to paperback for Createspace is something that you can definitely do yourself. It will take you anywhere from 30 minutes to two hours to convert the book. I have found a great resource that you can watch to convert the book yourself for free.

There is a great tutorial by author India Drummond on YouTube. The process will take you through how to convert it to Createspace. I also have created a free step-by-step guide that you can download at the end of this chapter that is based off of the tutorial. The only costs out of your pocket for the conversion are for the paperback book cover (usually around $25.00 on Fiverr) and your ISBN number, which you can purchase for $10.00 on Createspace.

For the book cover, I would recommend using the same freelancer that you use for your Kindle cover. My freelancer charges me $25.00, which I feel is a great value. You will need to decide what you want on the back of the book cover. I think it's a good idea to have your sales copy for your Kindle book on the back of the paperback cover.

Send that information to your freelancer so they can add it to your back cover. Another thing is that if you use your sales copy, make sure you take out any parts like "buy this now" at the top of the page. I made that mistake in the paperback book cover for Positivity Attracts and had to have my freelancer made the edits after the cover was already completed.

It will take a few days to get the book cover back from your freelancer as it is more work compared to the Kindle cover. Once you get the cover, purchase the ISBN, and have the conversion ready (don't forget to convert your converted Createspace ready word file to pdf) and then you can upload to Createspace.

You will also need to place the book in a book category on Createspace and it doesn't have to be the same as you chose on Kindle. You can choose something different if you would like. The categories will be a little different, so you might not be able to choose the same exact category anyway.

One final item that you will need to decide on is how much you want to charge for your book. All three of my books are prices at $9.99, and I have found that to be a good price point. My commission on that price point is $3.84 per book sold. At this point you will be able to get the book uploaded.

One of the best things about Createspace is that it works very quickly. Similar to ACX, you must have your Kindle ebook uploaded to Amazon and it must be live. Your Createspace book should be available on Amazon within 3-4 days.

In my view, having the book available as both paperback and Kindle creates several advantages. The first one is that you have several options for readers to choose from. There are people that do not want Kindle books, but do want paperback books. Having the paperback book will entice the reader who doesn't use Kindle to buy your book. The other part is perceived value.

The reader sees two prices when they go to your book page on Amazon. They will notice the print edition for $9.99 and in contrast will see your Kindle book for only $2.99. It is even better when your book is listed for free or 99 cents as it will also show how much you save with the Kindle edition. It will show 70 percent off when priced at $2.99 and 90 percent off at 99 cents.

I did not have a paperback edition of Eat Less and Move More ready until mid-September. However, I did notice when converting the book that I had a few errors in the Kindle version from my initial word file. I had my freelancer who does my Kindle conversions make a quick update so that I could have the errors fixed which were not caught at the initial launch.

With having paperback versions of both Motivation 101 and Positivity Attracts available when the books launched, I did see increased sales and at minimum I recommend having both paperback and Kindle versions available for when you launch.

__Download this step-by-step guide on www.brodieedu.com/resources to convert your book to paperback for Createspace__

Chapter 15 Building Your Email List

When I first heard the term funnel I was not clear on what it meant. After learning about this business over the past year, I learned the funnel is to move the readers who buy your books on Amazon to your email list.

Your goal is to funnel as many readers of your books as possible. That way, you can contact them yourself since Amazon is not going to give you the names of the readers who buy your books. The best way to get the readers funneled to your list is to give them something of value.

MailChimp is the list service that I currently use. It is free for your first 2000 people. After you reach 2000 you have to pay for the service. MailChimp is good, but they do not offer an autoresponder option for the free service. This is why I will be changing from MailChimp to AWeber prior to this book launch.

The AWeber service costs $19.00 per month and includes the autoresponder service. The autoresponder service is where you can set up three to four automatic e mails to readers who have just joined your list. It is a great opportunity to tell the reader about you and for you to give the reader some more gifts for joining your list.

There are other services but in my view MailChimp and AWeber are the best ones. As I plan to grow my list exponentially, I wanted to switch to AWeber while my list was still in the 200 range. I expect to have several thousand readers on my list by the end of 2016.

The reader list is your tribe so to speak. This list has made a connection to you through your writing and is interested in what you are offering. Building a large reader list is critical to an author's success and to their revenue streams.

Chapter 16 Lead Magnets

Lead magnets are what you will be giving away to your reader to get them to join your list. I use Lead Pages (costs $37.00 per month for the standard plan) to offer freebies to get readers. For that price you get virtually unlimited pages that you can create. You also do not need your own website as lead pages host the pages on their page. If you do have your own website, you can link the page to your website. For example, my free Motivation 101 audiobook is hosted on Lead Pages but is also available at www.BrodieEDU.com/FreeAudioBook.

My first freebie was created for the launch of my first book, Eat Less and Move More in August 2015. I actually wrote both Eat Less and Move More and version 1 of my second book, Motivation 101. Version 1 of Motivation 101 had my old cover, that I covered earlier in the book and was edited but was not a final copy.

It was a great lead magnet as I got over 100 readers to sign up to my list. In September 2015, I edited the lead page and changed out the free book of Motivation 101 to the free audiobook. I finalized Motivation 101 with a new cover and a final round of edits and launched the ebook on

Amazon in mid-September for an early October launch.

The audiobook of Motivation 101 was my new lead magnet and did well. We got another 50 people added to the list. For Positivity Attracts, I did not offer a new lead magnet but I did sent out an advanced PDF copy to my list through MailChimp. This was to give away something of value and to generate some sales as it was 99 cents prior to the free launch. Additionally, it generated several positive reviews, which is always great.

A strategy that I have learned from Kevin Kruse, the author of the amazing foreword of this book, is to make offers for each chapter of a book. You identify a theme in the chapter and offer something that correlates, then have all of the items in one bundle. You will notice that strategy in this book. What I realized is that there was a lot of additional information that I felt would be beneficial from contact information to my freelancers to guides to help with audiobook recording and book conversion and I wanted to offer it to you.

Having multiple offers in a book (like this one) greatly increases the probability of funneling the reader to your list. One of my most important goals is not only to build a great list of readers, but to always give people a lot of value for free. At times I will offer a service, such as my BrodieEDU Publishing Academy for Beginning Authors or coaching, but the main things I will be offering is freebies and free advanced copies of my books. That way, there is always value for the readers as I hope that many of you will take advantage of one of the offers in this book. The free audiobook of Motivation is also offered at the beginning of this book.

Chapter 17 Back End Products

The whole point of building your list is to be able to not only give great value to your readers but also to offer products otherwise known as back end products. I offer several including coaching and motivational speaking. Coaching has started to make me a considerable amount of revenue for me on the back end and my motivational speaking is projected to reach five figures for 2016. This was built up while teaching full time, so there is definitely time to build a business for you and a catalog of back end products that you can sell to your readership.

Webinars are another great way to promote your product or service. I will freely admit that I completely screwed up my first webinar product. I created a lead page and promoted it actively in the release of Motivation 101. I was selling a three part webinar for $49.99 (50 percent off the $99.99 price point). It would address three key components from the book with the first one covering Our Greatest Opponent. It failed miserably!

What I should have done was offer a FREE webinar and then sold my coaching service on the back end. I would have most likely made several hundred dollars minimum and it was a lesson learned. Sometimes products will sell really well, and sometimes they will fail.

I will most likely offer a free webinar in either the spring or summer of 2016, but I did put that isn't currently a priority for me. It was a great experience in what I learned. I know from this point the free webinar is the way to go and then to offer the upsell at the end of the webinar.

Another back end product that I will be pursuing in 2016 is creating several video courses on Udemy. Udemy is a great way for you to create an on-line course and have students sign up. It does take a lot of work to set up, but it is a great opportunity to make significant passive income as once your product is uploaded then you market it and start to build your business. My goal is to create multiple courses on Udemy with each course based on one of my books.

The potential on Udemy is to make hundreds of not thousands of dollars a month, but again it does take time. The best advice I can give to any author is to be patient. This is a marathon, not a sprint. It is definitely a process and it takes time. I have gone from making $150.00 on my first commission check, to now on pace for over $1000.00 a month from Kindle alone and that is since August 2015.

Again, this is mainly on Kindle sales with a couple hundred dollars from paperback and audiobook combined.

Chapter 18 Revenue Streams

In previous chapters, I have mentioned having multiple revenue streams. This is the key to becoming successful in any business and especially as an author. Having just a Kindle version in my view is not enough, especially with starting out. At minimum I highly recommend having both a Kindle and print edition of your book ready for each book launch. Below are potential revenue streams.

Kindle Edition of your book

Paperback Edition (Createspace)

Audiobook (ACX)

Public Speaking

Coaching

Book Signings

Udemy Courses

The paperback edition of your book is essentially the modern day business card. It is a great way to promote yourself and I highly recommend having several copies of each of your books with you, either in your car or in your backpack, purse, etc. I also recommend reaching out to bookstores where you live to see about book signings. They are a great potential revenue stream. You can typically buy your books from Createspace in bulk (around 100 copies) for around $250.00 to $300.00. If you end up selling 100 books at a book signing then your profit margin is potentially $700.00 on one successful book signing.

One thing that I do is have book signings at the end of my motivational seminars. I will offer either a package deal ($1000.00 for 100 books to sign) or sell them ala cart. It is a great way to bring in additional revenue and the investment is well worth it.

There are many revenue streams to utilize. These are a few that I hope will help you on your journey to becoming a bestselling author.

Conclusion

Through the past eighteen chapters we have covered a range of topics from editing your book, finding a great cover, writing a good book description, and ways to market your book. In addition, we also covered how to record your audiobook and convert your book to paperback, and the many potential revenue streams that are available. My hope is that this book can help with your own personal quest to become not only a published author, but a potential bestselling author.

I want to thank you for reading my fourth book. Writing each book is a labor of love. I write about things I am passionate about and I believe having a positive and motivated mindset is one of the most important things in life.

Stayed tuned for the release of my next book, The Pursuit of Happiness and I invite you to check out Eat Less and Move More, Motivation 101, and Positivity Attracts.

I would like to offer you the opportunity to read the first chapter of my next book publishing book. Click the link below to see the first chapter of Book Publishing for Authors.

Download the first chapter of Book Publishing for Authors at www.brodieedu.com/resources

About the Author

Paul Brodie is the President of BrodieEDU, an education consulting firm that specializes in the development of literacy programs, motivational seminars for universities and corporations, coaching, and wellness education. Brodie also serves as a Special Education Teacher for the Hurst-Euless-Bedford Independent School District.

From 2011-2014, Brodie served as a Grant

Coordinator for the ASPIRE program in the Birdville Independent School District. As coordinator, he created instructional and enrichment programming for over 800 students and 100 parents in the ASPIRE before and after school programs. He also served for many years on the Board of Directors for the Leadership Development Council, Inc with leading the implementation of educational programming in low cost housing.

Previously, Brodie spent many years in the corporate world and decided to leave a lucrative career in the medical field to follow his passion and transitioned into education. From 2008 to 2011, he was a highly successful teacher in Arlington, TX where he taught English as a Second Language. Brodie turned a once struggling ESL program into one of the top programs in the school district. Many of his students have moved on to journalism, AVID, art classes, and a number of the students exited the ESL program entirely. His methods included music, movies, graphic novels, and many high engagement methods including using technology, games, cultural celebrations, and getting parents involved in their children's education. Brodie's approach has been called unconventional but highly effective, revolutionary, and highly engaging.

Brodie earned an M.A. in Teaching from Louisiana College and B.B.A. in Management from the University of Texas at Arlington. Brodie is a bestselling author and has written four books. He wrote his first book, Eat Less and Move More: My Journey in the summer of 2015. Brodie's goal of the book was to help those like himself who have had challenges with weight. The goal of his first book was to promote not only weight loss but also health and wellness. He is also the author of Motivation 101 and Positivity Attracts. Both books are Amazon bestsellers and are based on his motivational seminars. His latest book, Book Publishing for Beginners will be available in January 2016. Brodie hopes the book will help people realize their dream of becoming a successful published author.

His motivational seminars have been featured at multiple universities and at leadership conferences across the United States since 2005. Brodie is active in professional organizations and within the community and currently serves on the Advisory Board for Advent Urban Youth Development and as a volunteer with the Special Olympics. He continues to be involved with The International Business Fraternity of Delta Sigma Pi and has served in many positions since 2002 including National Vice President –

Organizational Development, Leadership Foundation Trustee, National Organizational Development Chair, District Director, and in many other volunteer leadership roles. He resides in Arlington, TX.

Acknowledgments

Thank you to God for guidance and protection throughout my life.

Thank YOU the reader for investing your time reading this book.

Thank you to my amazing mom, Barbara Brodie for all of the years of support and a kick in the butt when needed.

Thank you to my awesome sister, Dr. Heather Ottaway for all of the help and feedback with my books and also with my motivational seminars. It is scary how similar we are.

Thank you to both Lise Cartwright and Kevin Kruse for writing incredible forewords for this book. It is an honor to consider you both not only fellow authors but also friends.

Thank you to Devin Hacker for serving as the editor of my fourth book. The slicing and dicing was very much appreciated and I could not have gotten this book published without her assistance.

Thank you to Lindsay Palmer who is working tirelessly to get me booked on college campuses · seminars throughout the United States. I could not have a better team of people to work with on Team Brodie.

Thank you to all who have served on the BrodieEDU Advisory Board.

Thank you to my dad, Bill "The Wild Scotsman" Brodie for his encouragement and support with the startup process of my books.

Thank you to Shannon and Robert Winckel (two members of the four horsemen with myself and our good friend, Derrada Rubell-Asbell) for their friendship and support. Shannon and Robert are two of my best teacher friends and are always great sounding boards for ideas.

Thank you to (Don) Omar Sandoval for his friendship and help with several BrodieEDU projects including building our awesome website.

Thank you to all of the amazing friends that I have worked with over the past twenty plus years. Each of them has made a great impact on my life.

Thank you to all of my students that I have had the honor to teach over the years. I am very proud of each of my kids.

Thank you to Delta Sigma Pi Business Fraternity. I learned a great deal about public speaking and leadership through the organization and every experience that I have had helped me become the person that I am today.

Thank you to my three best friends: J. Dean Craig, Jen Moorman, and Aaron Krzycki. We have gone through a lot together and I look forward to many more years of friendship.

Thank you to all of the students past and present at the UT Arlington and UT Austin chapters of DSP. Both schools mean a lot to me and I look forward to seeing them again at some point in the near future.

Thank you to the Lott Family (Stacy, Kerry, Lexi, and Austin) for their friendship over the past six years.

Thank you to Robin Clites for always taking care of things at the house with ensuring that Mom and I can always get that family vacation every year.

Contact Information

Interested in booking Paul for seminars, coaching, or consulting?

Paul can be reached at Brodie@BrodieEDU.com

Website www.BrodieEDU.com

Testimonials from Paul's seminar attendees

@BrodieEDU on Twitter

Paul G. Brodie author page on Facebook

Paul G. Brodie author page on Amazon

BrodieEDU Facebook Page

BrodieEDU YouTube Channel

Feedback

Please leave a review for my book as I would greatly appreciate your feedback.

I also welcome you to contact me with any suggestions at Brodie@BrodieEDU.com